WHICH OLD WOMAN WILL YOU BE?

Do's and Don'ts for Living Your ThirdThird on Purpose

Debbie Hensleigh

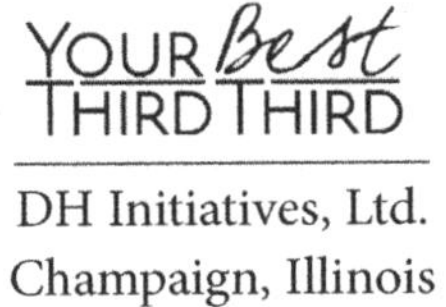

DH Initiatives, Ltd.
Champaign, Illinois

ISBN (e-book): 978-0-9997751-0-3
ISBN (print): 978-0-9997751-1-0

DH Initiatives, Ltd.
Debbie@Yourbestthirdthird.com
www.yourbestthirdthird.com

CONTENTS

CHAPTER ONE

THE PARTY

When I turned thirty-five, I suddenly felt like an adult.

At thirty-five, with five children, something came over me that said, "You are an adult, now. No matter how you feel or how you act. It has come." I splurged on an electric drip coffee maker, because anyone who is an adult should have their own, decent coffee maker.

When I was forty, my sisters and mother threw me a "surprise" birthday party in Austin, Texas. I had grown up in Austin and left when I was eighteen to seek my fortune elsewhere. I felt like I should go around and apologize to the family and friends who came to celebrate my forty years. I had grown and changed a lot over the twenty-two years since I left my family of origin and I cringed to think of how some of those people might remember me in my youthful, slightly wild years.

Another year, my kids decided I needed a party and with the help of a family friend, they pulled off another party that was a surprise. I was probably forty-three and I enjoyed a smaller, mostly family version of Birthday Party.

Then, I turned sixty in 2012.

I quit dying my hair.
I decided I wanted a party.

I had never really wanted a party before, but something came over me at sixty. I wanted a party and I wanted it a certain way:

At a local wine bar.

With appetizers.

And with a guest list prepared by me.

I told my husband what I wanted, where I wanted it, and who I wanted to be there. He was fine with that. He arranged everything. It was my party, so I didn't want to DO anything; I just wanted it done the way I envisioned it.

A few days before the party, my husband asked me about some people who were not on my guest list. "It's my party," I told him. "I only want the people I put on the list."

I had fun. I celebrated a milestone. I got what I wanted!

I tell people that when I turned sixty, I stopped dying my hair, I threw myself a party, and I got sassy.

That's pretty much what happened, in a nutshell.

❧ ❧ ❧

A few days after my sixtieth birthday party, I was thinking about being sixty years old.

Sixty seemed like slowing down.

Like arriving.

Like heading towards the finish line.

Like, maybe, thinking about retirement.

And then, I realized that my mother was ninety. Wow, ninety years old! Sixty (my age) to ninety (my mother's age) is thirty years. I could potentially live for thirty more years!

What am I going to do with THIRTY... MORE...YEARS? If I live to be as old as my mother, that's another third of my life!

The ThirdThird.

❧ ❧ ❧

My parents, part of the WWII generation, part of the "Greatest Generation," had a life expectation. They expected that they would work until they were sixty-five, then retire and travel for a few years, then die when they were about seventy-two. In fact, my mother had never, in as many generations as we can track, ever had a family member live beyond seventy-two years of age.

I, though, turning sixty in 2012, and firmly a Baby Boomer, should have every expectation that I just might live for a long time. With significant and ever-improving medical advancements and with more and better information on nutrition and health, we are all living longer.

> What does that mean?
> How should I plan?
> What will I do?

There's plenty of information on retirement planning and health care plans. Those details need to be attended to, but more important to me is:

> What am I going to DO with another thirty years?
> What will the ThirdThird of my life look like?
> What will I be like in my ThirdThird?
> What opportunities might be available to me?
> What responsibility do I have to live those thirty years well?
> What will I be like when I am ninety?

CHAPTER TWO

TWO KINDS OF WOMEN

I've thought about what I will be like as an old woman for a long time.

In 1980, I was the mother of three young boys, ages four, two, and a few months. We had moved to a new town far away from family, working with a student ministry. Our lives were full of people—young people, students, and peers. We were busy.

We also had almost no contact with anyone over the age of forty.

I was concerned that our children were growing up with a skewed view of the world. Not often around their grandparents or their one living great-grandmother, there were essentially no opportunities for them to be around older people and I was concerned that they would grow up to be uncomfortable with them.

I was intent on having our boys be comfortable around older people. Since I was at home with these boys and needed an outing myself, and assuming there were people in nursing homes who would enjoy visits from us, I contacted the local county nursing home and scheduled regular visits.

It was an adventure. The first day we ventured out, the four of us—my baby in a front pack and the other two ambling along—caught a bus, transferred to a second bus, and then walked a block to the county nursing home.

We were met by two women near the door:

> Woman #1 had a smile and a pocket full of butterscotch candies for the boys. She welcomed us and patted young heads. She tried to get the shy two-year-old to tell her his age. She engaged the 4-year-old.
>
> Woman #2 shuffled past and snorted when she was close enough for me to hear. She commented (loudly), "That baby should be able to hold his head up."

That son has Down Syndrome and her assessment stung. It was true, he couldn't hold his head up yet and we worked on that every day. It was an unkind comment and it made me wonder what I was doing in this place.

These two women were in the same circumstances: Elderly, unable to live alone, needing enough care that a nursing home was appropriate. They were both ambulatory, alert, and, most likely, had not anticipated a care facility as their dream home. I could imagine that they both had reason to be grumpy, depressed, and resentful.

But only one of them was.

These two women turned out to be a pretty fair representation of everyone there at that facility—both men and women.

> There were ones who engaged and ones who resisted.
>
> There were ones who welcomed and ones who shunned.
>
> There were ones who smiled and ones who frowned.
>
> The kind ones… *and the other kind of ones.*

Over the years, I have observed many people growing older. I often think back to those two old women, sitting near the door of the nursing home, being who they probably had been since they were younger.

That's the way it works with aging: we become more of who we really are as we grow older. We don't magically become someone else when we reach a certain birthday. A new, better personality does not get delivered with our Medicare card.

As we age, we become more of who we have always been. We care less what other people think of us.

I have had numerous "olders" tell me, "I know who I am and I'm not changing." That statement can be frighteningly true. As we age, we have less energy to pretend. When we are young, we can muster up the energy to smile and put on a happy face even if, at times, we don't really feel like acting happy.

As we age, that energy required to pretend to be someone other than who we really are is less easily appropriated. With less energy to pretend, with less concern of how we are perceived, we simply become more of who we have always been on the inside, at our core. Even if it has not always been evident who we really are.

As we age, we become…

> more thoughtful or more selfish.
> more generous or more miserly.
> more interested or more aloof.
> more patient or more distracted.
> more gracious or more bitter.
> more connected or more alone.

Unfortunately, we don't automatically become wise and gracious as we age. We don't magically become different people when we have grandkids or reach retirement age or become eligible for Social Security. We don't become wise and kind when our hair turns gray. No magic (poof!) makeover.

I have a friend who says she is sure that at a certain age, she will be the woman tied into her wheelchair and placed in the corner where she randomly spouts off bad words.

She has been holding in bad words for years. She is able to not say them in her second-third. She has the energy to put on a happy face (or at least to bite her tongue) and she doesn't want to offend or be thought of as coarse or rude. She figures she will reach a point where she is unable to hold all those naughty words in, though.

That picture disturbs me (even though with her, I can imagine it and we smile at the visual). I don't want to have something hidden in my life now that will surface at some time in the future when I am unable or unwilling to hold it in.

> Who I am now will be the largest part of who I am in the future.
>
> Who you are now, at your core, will engulf your existence at some point when you are old and can no longer hide it.

Our future is being determined by what we do in our present.

We can make choices now, daily, to ensure that when we are old women, we will be the woman we intentionally became. And by the way, you men out there, this applies to you too. You are choosing which old man you will be!

❧ ❧ ❧

The following chapters lay out seven Do's and Don'ts for you to consider. They are action points that can help you choose what you will be like, now and as you age—no matter which third of life you are in.

These do's and don'ts will help you in determining which "old woman" you will be when you have less energy to pretend and less concern of others' opinions—when the "real you" oozes out.

They can help guide your choices in how you live your life now, determining and intentionally designing your ThirdThird—so that you can live your ThirdThird on and with purpose.

Choose one of these Do's or Don'ts and begin to make it yours.

Then, choose another. And let it change you.

Start being that Old Woman you want to become…on purpose. Determine to live on purpose, intentionally forecasting which old woman you will become.

Which old woman will YOU be?

Or, which old man will YOU be?

CHAPTER THREE

DON'T COMPARE

We are so great at comparing ourselves to others, aren't we? The temptation is there. We can compare ourselves to people near us or ones we see on televisions or in magazines.

Do I look that old?

Do I have as many "friends"?

Do I weigh more?

Is my address better or worse?

Did I get invited, too?

Into my 60s, I was in a weight-lifting class where I was definitely the oldest member. I know that I tend toward competition, so I consciously tried to not compare the weight on my bar to the weight on the bars of the younger class members around me.

But I kept increasing my weights, telling myself I was only increasing to build strength and stamina, not to compete and look good compared to people less than half my age. Actually, I *was* comparing myself to the others in the class. But why? These people were the ages of my children!

In the 2.5 years I faithfully attended that class, the "aging process" began to catch up with me. I had a few aches and some nagging back soreness. Sometimes my hip hurt enough that I limped a bit until everything got "in place." I found a great massage therapist who I visited regularly to put me back in shape.

Then, I had a slight cold and I went on a trip over Christmas and I missed my weight lifting class for a few weeks. Lo and behold, aches abated. Back soreness was gone. No more limping. Hmm…maybe the source of my increasing pain and soreness was this particular class?

I switched to a yoga/tai chi/Pilates class.

I thought that it would be too easy to satisfy me, but that was not so! I was really sore after my first class of gentler bending and stretching instead of weight lifting and lots of reps. I was obviously using new muscles in new ways.

As I worked on the stretching and balance and flexibility that are focused in this class, I have minimized all that "aging" that was showing up as I pushed myself to keep up with others (even while trying to convince myself that I wasn't comparing myself to them).

Maybe I could do the weight-lifting class with lighter weights, but there was a lot of jerking and jumping that I have decided I can live happily without. The results of the yoga/tai chi/Pilates class are what I want.

The point is not the different class, but the fact that my comparing myself to others was killing me. We find many ways to compare ourselves to others and there are only two outcomes of that. Either

> …we will have an inflated view of ourselves, due to comparing to someone "less."
>
> or
>
> …we will have a lessened view of ourselves, due to comparing to someone "more."

The truth is...each of us, every one of us,

has our own brilliance,
our own beauty,
our own ability,
our own experience,
and our own story.

As we own all of who we are and who we are becoming, instead of comparing ourselves randomly to other people, we can learn from the brilliance and beauty and ability and experience and stories of those around us.

And as we see and appreciate other's great assets, we will grow ourselves. Since we naturally compare ourselves to others, here are some tips to avoid the temptation to compare.

Own Your Own Brilliance

I'm not saying you're perfect. But, if you know what you're good at and own it, you won't expect others to be brilliant in the same ways. Comparison, which will only distract you from your own brilliance, will be less of a temptation.

I had coffee recently with someone who is as far from "like me" as one could get. She was very put together. She was detail-oriented, for sure. She was smartly dressed and had the newest gadget on her phone. She was guarded and cautious in her conversation, thinking before she spoke. I enjoyed her. I learned some things from her. But, I didn't compare myself to her.

I am much more relaxed in my style. I am big-picture, dive-in-and-see-what-happens. I try to keep the same phone for as long as possible so I don't have to spend time with another learning curve.

If I had compared myself to her, I would have either berated myself for not being more classy or intellectual or tech savvy...or, I would have prided myself on not being as stuffy and prim. In either case, I would have lost out on a new friend and an opportunity to learn about things I now have some knowledge of.

By knowing yourself and owning your own brilliance, you can hold your own in a conversation. You can be genuinely interested in other people's stories and pick up ideas to use and expand on later.

It can feel like a big step to admit that you're NOT some ways. But you can't be good at everything. Focus on the ways that you can succeed and find enjoyment.

If you will know and own your own brilliance, you can be comfortable in your own skin without the temptation to compare yourself to someone else's brilliance.

Listen to Other Perspectives

I love conversation and I actually enjoy a good argument, if it is not emotionally charged and if there is respect on all sides. Exchanging opinions with explanations of "why" is a way to understand and to learn. Talking out the "why" is a learning/growing place.

I have a friend who is a therapist. She listens and empathizes and gives hope and strategy to her clients with skill. We became friends, and stay friends, intentionally.

I have been a coach and consultant for many years and while I listen and help strategize with my clients, I have a much different approach from my therapist friend. In general (and simplistically stated):

> *Therapists* tend to help their clients understand and deal with their past. *Coaches* tend to focus on where someone wants to go from here—the future.

Therapists are trained to understand and to work with the unconscious mind. *Coaches* tend to know and understand the conscious mind.

Therapists are problem oriented. *Coaches* are solution oriented.

Therapists ask more "when?" and "why?" questions. *Coaches* ask more "what?" and "how" questions.

My therapist friend and I have similarities, and we have occasionally recognized that one or the other of us might be more suited to help a particular client. But, we have different perspectives. What have I gained from having this friend whose brilliance is much different than mine?

I want to learn to be more patient and to understand why people do the things they do.

Why do we stay in relationships that are bad for us?
Why do we sink into gray hopelessness?
Why do we need other people to give us value?
Why do we not see our own brilliance?

As we meet and talk and exchange, I learn from my therapist friend.

What has my friend gained from our relationship? She wanted to learn to stop being taken advantage of, to say "no" when appropriate, and to balance her deep emotional care for others with a healthier skill of knowing when and how to challenge them to move forward.

This friend and I often seek one another out when we have a situation that puzzles or challenges us—she to ask how I would see things, and I to ask for her viewpoint. By listening to our different perspectives, we both grow.

It is a fading trait to hear and respect other peoples' perspectives. As we age, we store up more and more experiences and information. It is easy to form ironclad opinions that can stop us from seeing and hearing others. We tend to socialize with people who are similar to ourselves, and that tends to reinforce what we already think is true and good, and that can stop us, again.

It's easy to wall up, to quit listening, even to become angry when others disagree or have strongly-held, unyielding opinions.

"Help me understand."
"Why do you feel that way?"
"Tell me more."

These types of statements/questions help to open the door to understanding. You can use them to have conversations that could results in new friends and new ideas. The result of hearing others' perspectives can be that you find some of your own brilliance as you open yourself up to others experiences and references. And you can help someone else find their own brilliance.

If we only hear what we already think, chances are we will just become more like what we already are with little to challenge us to change and grow.

Find Opportunities to Honestly Say, "I Was Wrong"

When our children were teenagers, one of them pointed out to me that I never think I am wrong. "Hmm." Yeah. He was correct. Especially in conversations with our teen-aged children.

Comparing myself to the much younger offspring I was trying to train and guide and nurture made me pretty sure I was the "right one" in most of my conversations with these young ones. The reality, being entirely honest, is that I am, sometimes spot on.

And sometimes, I'm dead wrong.

Since this young man, who was often (and sometimes annoyingly) insightful, was bringing this to my attention, I determined that I should probably consider his perspective. I started to look for times I could honestly say, "I was wrong."

Admitting my mistakes does not necessarily make me feel immediately better, but it does clear the air, open relationships back up, and helps me to stand strong in the confidence that I can be wrong and human, yet still keep going forward and doing good. Sometimes, when appropriate, I even add, "You were right."

Saying, "I was wrong" communicates a lot.

> It communicates that honesty is important to me.
>
> It communicates that I value the relationships I am in.
>
> It communicates that I have a desire to keep growing and improving.

Admitting that you are wrong is good for the person you are apologizing to and it is really good for yourself as well.

For yourself, saying you made a mistake is a sign of strength. It is setting a good example of taking responsibility. It can lessen stress and improve relationships (personal truth).

For the person you apologize to, it can promote healing by giving them personal value and worth. It can promote understanding through communication. It is truly a gift given, a statement that the other person is important to you.

Saying, "I was wrong," is very constructive and at the same time, instructive. It is not always easy. But it is, often, very right and true. I was wrong and…

> I didn't know about that.
>
> I don't understand.
>
> I have not experienced that.
>
> I value my relationship with you.

A little side note here is that "but" is a verbal eraser, so saying "I was wrong but…" can negate any positive effect of the initial apology:

> "I was wrong to turn my back on you BUT you were being so idiotic I had to leave," is not exactly what I am talking about.

"I was wrong to turn my back on you" is enough said.

As you intentionally become who you want to be…
DON'T COMPARE.

Own your own brilliance.

Listen to others' perspectives.

Admit when you are wrong.

CHAPTER FOUR

BE INTERESTING

A great hobby I had at one point in my life was as a volunteer trip leader with Habitat for Humanity/Global Village. Habitat sells homes to families who meet specific criteria and who invest their own "sweat equity" into the homes they purchase. These homes are largely built with volunteer labor.

I led trips to Central America, Eastern Europe, and Central Asia. As a volunteer trip leader, my job was to organize, lead, facilitate, and manage a small team of 6–12 adults who wanted to "vacation with a purpose." I recruited volunteers from all over the United States with an occasional Canadian or European joining the team.

Experiencing the culture and food and building practices of Honduras and Armenia and Hungary and Kyrgyzstan and other places was worth every minute (hours and hours) of time before, during, and after the trips.

Spending 24/7 with an eclectic group of adults was fascinating. I was able to lead trips twice a year for a number of years. It was so interesting and very much out of my common experience.

Each trip was full of interesting (and sometimes annoying) people. During my time with Habitat, I met and worked with a slightly grumpy retired prison guard from Fresno, a boisterous single dad from Chicago, a thirty-something woman wandering the globe in search of herself, a twenty-something woman traveling on her own before committing to university, a 70-something Filipino tai chi master, a social worker from San Francisco with questionable sanity, and more.

Being in the same place for a week or two with complete strangers, and working on building a home for needy and deserving people was an amazing experience that broadened and improved me as a person. It was an enriching hobby that made me more interesting.

I am not leading trips at the present, but there are others ways to be interesting.

Find a New Hobby

Or, resurrect an old one.

I don't volunteer for the Habitat/Global Village trips any more, but I might in the future. Now, I am focusing on fitness and good, nutritious food as a hobby. I enjoy daily walking and/or yoga, new ingredients, staying fit and healthy.

I travel occasionally to interior Mexico with my husband to enjoy his business of taking travelers to wonderful places they may not venture to on their own.

And I would even say crossword puzzles are a hobby I have. I learn new words and find topics to learn more about almost daily from doing crossword puzzles.

What is a hobby you might try?

Did you have an interest and some ability in art class in Junior High? Buy a sketch pad or take a class and see if you still have it in you.

Did you once sew your daughters' dresses and make clothes for their dolls? There may be a need for heart pillows to be sewn and stuffed for the local hospital. I know a woman who retired and started making doll clothes and now has a successful small business. She loves going to craft shows and selling her creations.

Have you ever thought that you might enjoy learning a language or playing an instrument or singing in a community choir?

Take a class.
Join a choir.
Engage a teacher.

Love the outdoors?

Become a master gardener.
Find places to hike.
Buy a kayak.

Travel can be such a fun and rewarding hobby.

If you don't have a travel partner, find a way to go alone.
Try a service vacation with Habitat or a mission trip.
Join a group tour.

Do it. Try something. Be interested in something. Find a new hobby to be interesting.

Keep Up with Current Events

World news can be depressing, as can local news. But it is the world we live in and if you know what is going on around you, you are more interesting.

And, there is a lot going on around us that is neither depressing nor distressing. Neither political nor polarizing.

Life being lived by millions of humans:

Inspiring stories.
Clever solutions.
Fascinating possibilities.
Fun stuff.

Keeping up with the world in general or in specific will keep you interesting and open all sorts of doors to keep learning and growing.

Podcasts

Podcasts are audio files that are available on your computer, tablet, or cell phone apps—on any subject you might be interested in. Many are available as a series, with weekly installments, that you can subscribe to.

There are many regular podcasts on business development, personal improvement, political discussion, religious topics, etc. You can find well-informed and note-worthy podcasters by searching the Internet, or an app on your cell phone.

NPR has a number of interesting possibilities that include long stories with several episodes. It's sort of like watching a really good movie or reading a novel while walking or doing dishes when you have your headset on and are listening to a podcast. (www.npr.org/podcasts)

You can also help beginner podcasters and/or bloggers who are interested in similar topics to you by subscribing and commenting on their efforts. New podcasts are appearing every day!

TED Talks

TED talks are short videos of speakers talking about a variety of subjects. If you want to hear about space travel or medical advances or how laughter is healing or how shame can be overcome, there is a TED talk for you. To find a TED talk that interests you, go to www.ted.com, or download the TED app on your cell phone.

Local News and Newspapers

We have taken the local newspaper for years. It is where I get my daily crossword puzzle! There is just something about a newspaper delivered every morning to our home that I enjoy.

It is obvious that in the past few years, the publisher of our local paper has become very intentional about focusing on local human-interest stories. I am pretty sure it is a good way to sell papers. A young colleague of mine was recently in the paper and I brought him a copy to send to his grandmother. "How'd you know she told me to send her one," he asked. Ha! Of course his grandmother wanted to see her grandson's accomplishments in print.

I see people I know in the paper often, so I can comment on it when I run into them. It makes me seem interesting if I am focusing on their story!

> "You had an anniversary!"
> "Your granddaughter got an award!"
> "I saw that your organization raised money and had an event."

Noticing and commenting on local involvement is a way to be interesting.

Volunteering

You can volunteer with your local government to stay informed about local issues. Cities have all sorts of Action Committees that need good, thinking, and interested participation. In our town, there are…

- Board of Fire and Police Commissioners
- Library Board
- Telecommunications Commission
- Code Violation and Review Board
- Historic Restoration Commission
- Human Relations Commission
- Neighborhood Services Board
- Planning Commission
- Zoning Board of Appeals

All are open to citizens applying for membership.

Learning about your local community and finding ways to be involved is a way to be interesting, since many residents don't know about these opportunities. There are local needs and causes that are looking for people to help promote and sustain them. It just might be interesting to learn more about one of them.

However you like to get information, do it. Get true details. Listen, watch, read. Know what's going on.

Have Relationships with People Who Are Not the Same as You

It is easiest to be with people who are like you, and who you already know. You agree. You move along at the same pace. You probably have enough history to be able to avoid stepping on each other's toes.

To be interesting, though, mix it up a little. Talk to someone you don't know well.

> A neighbor who walks their dog past your home daily.
>
> The woman browsing in the same aisle you are.
>
> The man waiting in line with you at the Post Office.

It might help to have some conversation starters that you are comfortable using. Think about it and plan ahead to speak to someone new. Questions are good. So are compliments. Here are some suggestions:

> What kind of dog is that? Have you had it long? He certainly seems to enjoy his daily walks. (For the neighbor you see regularly but have never spoken to.)
>
> Have you tried this product before? Would you buy it again? Is there one you like better? (For the shopper in the same aisle.)
>
> What is your secret for staying so patient? (For the young mother wrestling the three-year-old in the parking lot.)

Arrange a lunch date with someone you haven't seen for a while. Or, meet them for a glass of wine or cup of coffee, or, arrange for them to come to your home for a meal.

Reconnect with Someone You Enjoyed in the Past

I recently received an email from a long-ago friend who had moved away. We sort of stayed in touch, but eventually, there was little connection. Once Facebook came along, we became "friends" again and were at least able to see photos of each other's kids who we had known well.

One day, she reached out and said she was going to be driving through our town and wondered if we could have coffee. Yes! It was so good to catch up and reconnect and remember the fine friendship we had long ago.

Get To Know Someone from a Different Culture

Nearing retirement, in her 60s, my mother joined "Friendship International" a volunteer organization serving international women and children in Austin, Texas. The leaders of the organization asked if she wanted to teach a class on idioms. "Sure" she said. And then, "What's an idiom?"

She taught that class for 25+ years and had friends and "second daughters" all over the globe. When we were downsizing her home, there were a lot of gifts that she had received from many different countries. Hearing her relate how she received them was interesting.

Learn about someone else's family traditions.

Go to lunch with someone with different dietary preferences than you.

Engage someone you would usually simply pass by.

Say hello or give a compliment.

Meet a stranger.

Force yourself to have a conversation with someone with different political views.

Listen to them and ask questions for understanding.

There is a room of stories in a room of strangers. Exchanging stories is rich. Be willing to share your story and to listen to others' stories.

You never know who you might meet. These conversations and experiences don't have to lead to new best friends or even regular friends.

Having experiences with different people will stretch you.

And make you better.

And you will be interesting.

As you intentionally become who you want to be...
BE INTERESTING.

Have an interest.

Know what's going on.

Let there be diversity.

CHAPTER FIVE

REFUSE TO BE LONELY

We are designed to have connection with other humans and there is a lot of evidence that lack of social contact is bad for us. Not only can loneliness lead to depression and alcoholism, but it also can affect our health by creating high blood pressure and can impede learning and memory. Solitary confinement will wreck your life. It is the severest form of punishment.

Don't do it to yourself.

After my husband, Dave, retired, he started a travel business. In his search for what to do next, he found himself in Copper Canyon, a majestic area in the Sierra Nevada Mountains in northern Mexico. Copper Canyon is a series of seven canyons that are longer and deeper than the Grand Canyon.

Dave became completely enamored with the canyons and the people and the food and the only passenger train in Mexico. The train, El Chepe, travels through the canyons from Chihuahua City to the Sea of Cortez.

I say that Dave went to Copper Canyon and fell in love. So much does he love Copper Canyon and Mexico, that he wanted to take other people there to experience this magical place.

He created Authentic Mexico Travel. To be authentic himself, he needed to spend time enough in the area to refresh his Spanish, meet, hire, and train top-notch, local guides and to find the best vendors and destinations. He spent a LOT of time in Mexico, researching hotels and restaurants, locating the most enjoyable of everything in Copper Canyon and making new friends (some of whom are now like family).

All this while I was at home in the good old USA, running a real estate company.

Dave and I have been married a long time and we are comfortable companions. We enjoy walking 1.5 miles to downtown to eat out. We enjoy being out of doors and recently bought kayaks. We enjoy projects (like flipping houses or remodeling our home or mowing and clearing land that we own by the river). We like to travel to Chicago by car or train for a weekend in the big city. We love an occasional Cubs game.

When Dave was traveling a lot, I found myself *not* doing some things I wanted to do because I was alone. Without Dave, I sat at home, making a list of things I would have gotten him to do with me, IF he had been home. (How crazy is that!?)

> I realized I was lonely.
>
> And I didn't need to be.

I started making intentional effort to get out and do and see and taste at home while Dave was doing and seeing and tasting in Mexico without me. I needed to learn to refuse to be lonely.

Look for Someone Else Who Needs to Not Be Lonely

An easy target for me with finding someone else who needed to not be lonely is our son, Joel, who happens to have Down Syndrome. Joel is an adult and he lives with us (or, he would say, we live with him). He is pretty independent, works at the local YMCA keeping score for men's noon basketball and keeping the workout area clean. He also works at the Park District in the summer, taking care of animals at a small farm/petting zoo. He has friends and plays sports and can get just about anywhere he wants to be by bus or on foot.

Joel loves to eat out. He will try new foods when he is out of the house, branching out from his own cooking which tends to focus on tortillas and beans and salsa. So, Joel and I have started some while-Pop's-out-of-town traditions. One is "Dollar Sushi night." Dave isn't keen on sushi and Joel has discovered he likes it, so sushi night is an easy choice. Recently, Joel discovered he likes Indian cuisine, so there is new exploring to do. Getting out of the house and trying new foods is good for both of us.

Besides Joel, I have a client who is widowed and who also loves to try new restaurants. She is fascinating, with her stories of growing up in Germany, and then living all around the world with her husband and children. The flat in Paris, the palace in Iran, the favorite home in Australia are stories I want to hear more about. She is a ready lunch companion and we keep each other from thinking we might be lonely.

And I have single friends. Or married friends whose husbands are out of town or who enjoy a night at home while their wives go out with friends.

Dinner out,
a concert in the park,
a glass of wine after a City Council meeting,
a movie.

There is no need to sit home alone and feel lonely while there are other humans around!

Attend an Event Alone

When I was figuring out for myself that I should not be spending all my non-working time alone, I thought of my mother.

My mother and daddy met in junior high and were each other's one and only love. They were married almost forty years until his untimely death from a heart attack at age sixty-one.

Unexpectedly to her, my mother lived for 30-plus years after she was widowed. She was a very social being and she certainly learned not to stay at home and be lonely.

She had tons of friends. She lived in the same city for virtually all her life (minus a short stay with relatives during the Great Depression). She was in a Birthday Club for years and attended church faithfully. After retiring, she found ways to volunteer and made more friends along the way.

As the years went on, Mother, naturally, had more and more widow friends, and they were always on the go—eating out, attending concerts, visiting hobby shows, playing cards or "42" (a Texas domino game). She rarely needed to attend anything alone.

There came a time, though, that her friends were less willing or able to "go." She stayed strong and relatively healthy for a long time, outlasting many of her previous partners in activity.

As others slowed down and were less available, did she stay at home? No way. If no one else was available and she really wanted to go, she would go alone. And, invariably, she would find someone to connect with—someone she knew or someone new for her to know.

It is so tempting to stay at home and be lonely and watch something on television or one of the many internet options for entertainment. But some movies are just better if they are seen on the big screen. It is entirely possible for you to go alone.

I have a list of a few artists who I would absolutely go see alone if no one else was interested or available and the opportunity arose. I'm not a great concert-goer, but for these, I have pre-determined that I would go alone:

Tommy Emmanuel
Yoyo Ma
Willie Nelson
Temple Grandin (not an artist, but a fascinating speaker)

Since I know it is tempting to forgo something I would really enjoy simply because I don't want to go alone, I am preventing any regret by deciding beforehand that I won't miss out.

Wandering a holiday craft show alone might actually be better than going with someone else. Having to pay attention to items that someone else is interested in that you have no appreciation for can be tiring.

Attending a lecture or signing up for a class that might help you grow or learn is certainly worth the effort of going alone.

Sitting at home, being lonely, makes you miss out on a lot that you don't have to miss out on. If you have been used to having a companion, going alone can feel strange. But, if you really want to see it, do it, experience it, then, get past the fear of being alone and attend an event all by yourself.

Refuse to be lonely.

Have Relationships That Include Truth and Laughter

I have a longtime friend in another city who was putting her life and marriage back together after finding out that her husband had an affair. She called me almost every day for a long period. She felt safe with me. She used me to give her perspective. And every time we talked, we laughed about something.

In an incredibly stressful time in her life, she needed to remember that there is joy in life. She needed to have a friend to laugh with who would also tell her the truth.

On the other hand, another woman in her 70s joined one of my Habitat for Humanity trips. This woman could not laugh at anything, though other trip members did regularly. She didn't seem concerned with the truth in situations. She could only see things from her own perspective. She was a daily challenge and alienated even the most tolerant of team members by trip's end. One wondered why she ever left home since she appeared to be miserable almost constantly, even though she said she loved Habitat trips.

Post-trip reflection helped me understand why she said she loves Habitat trips. After two weeks with her, observing the effect she had on the people around her and experiencing her outlook, I suspect she doesn't have a relationship with anyone who will agree to spend two weeks with her. So she travels with strangers, people who do not know her well enough to speak truth to her. People who are kind to her and who include her for two weeks, but who are very glad they live a continent away from her. People who would laugh with her if she could find any joy. In retrospect, I can see that she was lonely. That's why she couldn't laugh.

Find ways to be with people who will tell you the truth and laugh with you.

> "Uh, I don't want to alarm you, but did you know you have on two different earrings?"
>
> "Remember the time you thought that person was being funny and laughed when they really were telling you about a serious situation? This might be another of those times."
>
> "You might be seeing things only from your own perspective on this."
>
> "Tell me again about the time your friend lost his emu." (True story)

Find ways to be with people...

> who will listen to you complain, but then remind you that your boss is no more frustrating than other bosses are.
>
> who will make you laugh at yourself after telling you that you are too grumpy.
>
> who will remind you that you were excited when you first met your spouse.
>
> who will alert you to the fact that you have salad in your teeth.
>
> and who will tell you that it's time for you to take a vacation.

Laughter that comes from understanding and history and authenticity is wonderful evidence of acceptance. It might take some work and time and patience to find others who will carve a relationship with you that is marked by grace and truth and laughter. And there may be only a few relationships in your life that are truly like what I am describing.

I call these my "hot fudge sundae" friends. I prefer them and would love to exclusively do life with them but that is not realistic—or healthy. Life is full of all sorts of relationships, but it is worth the work and the wait for those few who are the "hot fudge sundae" relationships.

Find friends who will tell you the truth and who will laugh with you.

Build relationships so that you have options beyond traveling with strangers.

As you intentionally become who you want to be…
REFUSE TO BE LONELY.

Find someone who needs a friend.

Go somewhere alone.

Live with truth and laughter.

CHAPTER SIX

BE A READER

Some of us were born readers. You know who you are—you read the back of the shampoo bottle if there is nothing else to read in the bathroom.

You keep a stack of books by your bed. You read fiction, non-fiction, biographies, magazines, blogs, newspapers, even encyclopedias (maybe, or, at least you used to!).

Others of us have to learn to be readers. Your first inclination is not to pick up the printed page, but to find something else to do besides read. Sitting in a comfy chair, enjoying the feel of turning pages, or wandering through the stacks at the library are unknown pleasures.

Reading is an important part of personal growth and broadening as an individual. It can make us interesting and give us something to think about other than ourselves.

I have been a reader since I was old enough to read. I love to read. I am convinced I am bowlegged from sitting too long on the bookmobile floor when I was in grade school with my knees together and my feet back to the sides, finding more Beverly Cleary books or wishing that Madeline L'Engle had written more, or that the Boxcar Children were in my neighborhood.

Whether you are a born reader or not, there are some sound reasons to read more.

Read to Discover New Interests

My husband and I subscribe to a new magazine every year or so and only subscribe to the number of magazines we can read thoroughly. So, we are changing things up regularly.

One year, it was *Fast Company, Newsweek, Real Simple,* and *Cooking Light.* Another year, it was *Inc., Time, The Economist,* and *Food and Wine. Wall Street Journal, Clean Eating, Condé Nast Travel, Runners World,* and *Prevention Magazine* all have found their way into our rotation, along with others.

By mixing it up, we find...

> new recipes to try.
> new places to research.
> new medical information.
> new projects and approaches.

Varying our reading helps us find new interests. It makes us consider new and interesting places we might visit. It makes us curious about movies to see and more books to read. We tear pages out of magazines that have recipes we want to try, to increase the odds that we will actually try them.

I like reading stories. I find that historical novels are interesting and teach me about history in just about the only way I've ever enjoyed learning the essential lessons that looking back afford. I mix it up by seeking out different eras to read and learn about. Recently, I read a biography about a runner (Louie Zamberini) and ended up learning about Japanese WWII war prisons. *The Physician* took me through the 11th century...definitely not a common source of interest for me.

A high school classmate of mine recently published a novel set in the Civil War and I bought and enjoyed it, and learned that Rebel and Yankee soldiers often switched sides.

I read the *Little House on the Prairie* books to my kids, as well as Rebecca Caudill books, about the early settlements in the U.S. They are now reading them to their children and helping them become interested in another life, another time.

To inspire interest in our children's lives, Robert Clyde Bulla was another author for read-aloud time in our home when our kids were little. I remember once picking up Johnny Tremain for one of our boys, reading the first chapter to be sure it was not too difficult for him (it was) and becoming so enthralled that I read it aloud to Dave.

My husband and I occasionally find a book we're both interested in and I will read it to him. Most recently, it was a novel about Frida Kahlo that prompted a visit to a museum of her and Diego Rivera's art in Mexico City. Before that book, "Kahlo" was just an occasional answer to a crossword clue.

Reading can take you to new places and open you up to new ideas and people on a regular basis. One piece of advice, though: don't keep reading a book that doesn't interest you. There are plenty of others out there that will connect with you. Don't waste your time on a book that doesn't hold your attention.

Read to Make Connections with Other People

I had a coach who gave me a new slant on reading. He explained to me that he reads so he can be interested in other people, and have meaningful conversations with people he meets. What a great reason to read! Focused on others, but enhancing himself, he reads for connection and for understanding.

With that attitude, he does not limit himself to a topic or genre, but reads all sorts of things so that he can connect with other people. Reading to connect and to understand is a way to keep your own mind sharp and open.

We have all been around someone who is a one-pony-show: One topic to discuss, one interest to share, one experience to tell (again and again).

And we all know that gets tiring pretty quickly.

In contrast, the people who are connected are the ones who know how to talk about topics that other people are interested in.

You don't have to be an expert. Maybe you only know enough to be genuinely interested. Being genuinely interested is a great way to engage.

My husband, Dave, was not a reader until a bit later in his life. Someone recommended a list of books for him to read, informing him that "readers are leaders." One of the first books he read was *Life is Tremendous* by Charlie T. Jones. It made him realize a positive attitude helps in relationships. It was an attitude adjuster.

Later, Dave had a mentor who told him he read a book a week. "Dave, you will be exactly the same a year from now except for the people you meet and the books you read," he encouraged.

Now, Dave is a reader. He reads novels and he studies nonfiction and he peruses periodicals.

Reading current events, studying topics that interest, browsing periodicals, and scanning the local newspaper, and online blogs makes you interesting to talk to. If you are interesting to talk to, you will make new connections.

Read to Keep Up with Local Events

Our local community has had some pretty interesting situations. In a recent election, there were four people running for mayor, seven running for school district positions, in an almost complete turn-over, as well as park district board challenges and a referendum or two.

By keeping up with local drama, conversations were fun and people were interested (and entertained) to talk about the issues. I told my friend who was running for mayor (successfully) that if you didn't care about outcomes, it was pretty entertaining to live in our community. (She informed me that we do care about outcomes!)

Keeping up with local events was a fun way to be interesting and to have good conversations. I often remind myself that "You never know when the next person you meet will change your life forever."

If I'm interesting and have an interest in other people, the odds of meeting someone who might be impacted by me or have an impact on me grows tremendously.

Read to stretch your imagination. Reading takes you places, teaches you things, and tells you how to be innovative and how to keep growing.

Books and Authors that Have Impacted My Life

Today, the top five books I've read are: *Jane Eyre, Christy, The Purpose Driven Life, Memoirs of a Geisha,* and *The Kite Runners.*

From these, I discovered that...

> I actually can be a romantic.
> I want my home to be a refuge and place of comfort.
> I want to be confident in what I believe and why.
> There are unbelievable obstacles women can overcome.
> Cultures are deep and full and very multi-dimensional.

I said five, but I will go on and mention, *Three Cups of Tea, The Lacuna, The Chronicles of Narnia, The President's Lady* and *Mr. Audubon's Lucy.* I enjoy novels written by George McDonald, John Grisham, Patricia Cornwell, (Scarpetta) and Maeve Binchy.

Some of those books were vacation reads. Others have had lasting impact. Some gave me great escape and relaxation. Others motivated me to reach out to touch another life.

I read *The Chronicles of Narnia* to our children multiple times and they learned to imagine and visualize by listening the descriptions and narrative of the amazing and creative mind of C.S. Lewis.

I have nonfiction favorites, too:

> Any of John Maxwell's books on leadership
> *One Minute Manager* by Ken Blanchard

Five Dysfunctions of a Team by Patrick Lencioni
When Fish Fly by Joseph Michelli and John Yokoyama.

There have been life-changing books that caused me to think in new ways or to dramatically change directions.

One is *The Dip* by Seth Godin, which was actually a catalyst for major adjustments for my husband and me, including (but not limited to) changing jobs and relocating to a new state, 11 hours away from our long-time home town.

Younger Next Year (for Women) by Chris Crowley and Harry S. Lodge, M.D., has prompted significant daily alterations for me and my husband (who prefers the original book, *Younger Next Year*). This book motivated us to move from casual to intentional about daily exercise and become even more serious about our diets. We are now focused on making sure we do all we can to stay fit and active into our 80s and beyond.

Books have helped me imagine my life differently. They show me how others live and what others overcome and what trips others up.

I learn from reading books—both fiction and nonfiction. One of the few regrets I have is that I have not kept a list of all the books I have read. It would have been so easy to add those titles into the journals I have kept for most of my life.

My advice is: read books that teach good lessons that are well-written. Don't just escape—explore! Be discriminate with your time.

Reading will keep your mind sharp.
It will give you something to talk with others about.
It can get you thinking about larger issues.
It can make you smile and weep and empathize and wonder.

Some studies even show that reading reduces stress and can slow your heartbeat. Take a "reading vacation." You don't have to go anywhere or spend anything. Just block out some time to "go somewhere" by reading a book.

As you intentionally become who you want to be…
BE A READER.

Discover new interests.

Find ways to connect with other people.

Stretch your imagination.

CHAPTER SEVEN

DON'T BE BORING

Old women with nothing to do and nothing to talk about and nothing to contribute are not pleasant to be around. It's even worse when they are boring, talking about only themselves!

An article in *Fast Company*, a few years ago, stated the statistic that "people who live to be 85 have a 50-50 chance of becoming senile." The suggested remedy was to keep learning new things. Learning new things, beyond helping to avoid senility, certainly can help at not being boring so that we aren't the women avoided by others. The article went on to say that we generally think that if we are active, we are continually learning, but that is not necessarily true.

Learning new things is different than being active: *It takes intention.* To keep from declining mentally, we need to activate the learning potential in our brains. In the article, one scientist suggested learning Spanish or learning to play the oboe to keep the brain active and not stagnant.

If you don't want to be boring, you don't have to tackle a subject that you aren't interested in to generate more brain cells or to keep the ones you have. You don't have to change who you are. You just have to keep your curiosity working and keep finding new things that you can be genuinely interested in.

To keep from being boring, I need to be learning new things. I have a strong personality and generally know what I think about something.

That in itself is not necessarily interesting; in fact, it's probably not at all interesting to some.

I have found that a great way to learn new things is to be interested in other people and what they are learning, rather than just telling others what my opinions are.

Be who you are in a more interesting way. Start with baby steps if this is a new thought. Try one new way to keep from being boring.

Be Interested in Other People's Stories

Dale Carnegie in his book, *How to Win Friends and Influence People,* talks a lot about making other people feel important. We all like to talk about ourselves more than anything else, so getting others to talk about themselves makes you not boring…IF you are perceived to be truly interested.

How do you become (or act like) you are interested in others? Find a topic that you share. It's like playing catch. Listen, ask. Ask, listen.

That reminds me of another favorite children's book series, *Soup,* by Robert Newton Peck. In one book, a teacher explains that conversation is like playing catch. I throw the ball to you, you throw it back to me. That's another great read-aloud book if you have a young one to read to. It is also worth a quick read for yourself if you need a smile.

Ask "how?" and "why?" more than "what?" or "when?" A simple twist of common questions can lead to more interesting conversation.

> "How did you find your job?" to follow up "where do you work?"
> "How do you know [our mutual friend]?"
> "Why do you serve on this Board?"
> "What interests you about the topic of tonight's presentation?"

More to talk about!

We used to have a custom around our dinner table when we had guests. Before our children could leave the table after the meal, they had to ask a question to learn from or about our guests. It could not be a yes-or-no or one-word-answer question.

Children are clever and they quickly came up with "...and why?" as a way to stimulate more words.

> "When did you come to this country...and why?"
>
> "What is your favorite color...and why?"
>
> "How many kids do you have...and why?"

If all five of our children were at home and around the table, by the time it came to the last one, the questions got a little more creative (or not). But they definitely got conversation going. We learned a lot about a lot of people. And we learned not to talk only about ourselves.

When you start being interested in the people around you, there is no limit on how you might be changed.

In one of my work situations, we started a monthly potluck. Because there were a number of ethnicities and nationalities represented, the meals were really interesting. As we asked, we learned about cultures and lives that we would never have known.

> Rice balls from Singapore brought a really sweet story about a girl and her mother.
>
> Yellow kiwi shared brought news of a visiting Korean mother.
>
> Chicken and noodles were a shared family holiday favorite.
>
> Matcha tea, white chocolate cheesecake created by a computer techie, was met with enthusiastic appreciation, and proved to be the beginning of monthly new flavors.

At least one realized dream resulted from co-workers who took the time to sit together at a meal once a month to be interested in one another:

the cheesecake experiments actually grew into a small business. One cheesecake, then another. Interest grew as we heard the dreams of our coworker because we asked questions and showed genuine support for more cheesecakes!

Ask More Interesting Questions

If you want to be an interesting (i.e., not boring) person to be around, learn to ask better questions. When you are going to be in a situation with others, prepare by thinking up some new responses to make or questions to ask. How often, when someone asks you how your day is, do you think they are actually interested in how your day is going? Probably, not often.

Do you get to the point that you don't even answer the question "How are you?" because you're not sure they'll still be listening if you do? Instead of assuming others don't care and risking becoming cynical (the "other kind of woman"), think sincerely about how you might truthfully and positively answer "how are you?" A popular radio personality says, "Better than I deserve."

My husband often answers with a percentage that usually at least produces curious second consideration. "I'd say about 89%" sounds like a good day. I have developed the habit to respond by saying, "I have no complaints." More often than not, it is met with a chuckle and, "Nobody would listen anyway!"

It is worth it, if you want to be interesting, to spend some thought to come up with some sincere, but new, questions to ask of your friends and/or new acquaintances.

> "What's the best part of your week, so far?"
>
> "How do the host(ess) and you know one another?"
>
> "Why did you choose your profession?"
>
> "What do you enjoy doing in your free time?"
>
> "Is there something you're working on that you are excited about?"

As you show deeper interest in other people's lives, they will be more interested in yours.

This idea of asking better questions to be interested in someone else takes thought and practice. There is danger in asking a question that might be considered too personal. There is also danger in asking a question that you don't really care about.

There are some people who are just natural at putting people at ease and drawing them out in a way that makes everyone feel good. If that is not your most natural trait, then watch and learn from the people around you who are good at it. There are people around you who do have that trait, and you can learn from them.

Being sincerely interested in someone else is a learned skill. Maybe it is even part of good character. As a bonus, if you can learn to ask good questions and encourage meaningful and positive conversation, you will become more interesting as you consider your own questions for yourself.

Be Engaged

Have you ever tried to carry on a conversation with someone who is constantly scanning the room to see who else might be around? Or, have you been in a situation where one person was completely dominating the conversation so that you, or someone else, could never get a word in edgewise? Of course you have. We all have.

I used to get really annoyed with people who wouldn't stay focused on me—until I noticed that I tended to do the same thing when I was in a crowd of people.

> Weddings (who might show up that I haven't seen in years?)
>
> Conferences (who is near that I would like to connect with?)
>
> Dinners at restaurants (who might be coming in that I would or would not like to see?)
>
> Even church!

Since it is so annoying to me, and since I realized that without intentional thought I do the same thing, I do all I can to purposefully focus on the person I am speaking with. No wandering eyes or scanning allowed. I even try to remember good body language, such as to keep facing towards the person without crossing my arms.

It's not always easy, but I consciously work hard to stay focused for as long as I am there with that person.

I find that a lot of people notice my focus in my conversation with them and they appreciate it. Being engaged is also that exchange of words mentioned before, like playing catch.

My husband and I were recently in one of the most awkward situations we have been in for a long time when we were seated at a table with one person who talked incessantly. And I am not exaggerating.

I, being my conversational self and wanting to be interested in everyone at our table, tried several times to interject a comment or ask someone else at the table a question. After several valiant, but unsuccessful, attempts, I gave up. We ate our food and excused ourselves, vowing to remind each other to avoid that person in social situations in the future.

Though I am sure this man was trying to be engaging, he was boring! And, I am pretty sure, not just boring to Dave and me.

Interaction is interesting; monopolizing is boring—no matter how interesting the monopolizer thinks they are.

> Engaging with others can be
> entertaining,
> enlightening,
> enjoyable.

When we focus on the person in front of us and ask interesting questions and listen with intention, we will definitely not be boring.

Of course, at times, we are in a conversation with someone who is not all that interesting, but they still deserve the respect of undistracted engagement.

I find that it is always good to have a plan for polite escape—a statement or need that is genuine yet dis-engaging. Being engaged doesn't mean being controlled by someone else. Being engaged is simply focused attention for as long as the conversation is meaningful.

But still, maybe an annoying, engaged conversation might be better than sitting at home alone if your goal is to be an interesting and enjoyable person yourself.

As you intentionally become who you want to be...
DON'T BE BORING!

Be interested in others' stories.

Ask interesting questions.

Engage.

CHAPTER EIGHT

KNOW YOUR PURPOSE

A central focus in my work is helping people design a "Life on Purpose." We are living longer and should really be planning on living into our nineties.

That's a long time to wonder what we are supposed to be doing, whether it is another forty years or another thirty years or another twenty years. It takes some intentional thought and practice to narrow down all the possible ways we can spend our time and invest our energy.

> If you know what is important to you,
> what you value,
> and how you are wired,
> you can focus on things that will give you satisfaction.

Having focus allows you to avoid those tasks and people who are energy drains. It allows you to say "yes" or "no" with a reason, and to be able to wisely choose opportunities that energize and interest you.

With focus, you can say "no" without guilt, because you know why you are opting for "this" and not "that."

One of my popular workshops is "Life on Purpose." The end result of the workshop is to write a personal mission statement.

One of the exercises in Life on Purpose focuses on values and qualities. Participants choose and rank 10 values and 16 personal qualities in order of importance to them.

> Is "experiencing love and affection" more or less important to you than "family cohesiveness?"
>
> Do you rank "financial security" above or below "good health?"
>
> Is "personal power" or "personal freedom" what you would choose as more important?

It is a great exercise to go through—and harder than people expect. It's good hard work, though. Understanding what you value and defining the personal qualities that you hold dear gives clarity and direction for determining your "life on purpose."

Long ago, I was at a women's early morning Bible study with other twenty-somethings when a young woman said, "I can't wait until I am a wise, older woman." I remember thinking at the time, "We can't just assume that we will be wise when we are old?"

It's not like wisdom will come with our Medicare card.

This young woman knew that she valued wisdom. But it would be naive to think that she would just one day become wise without consciously applying herself to learn wisdom.

I'm pretty sure we all thought we were wiser than we actually were at twenty-something. But that morning, I realized I needed to be consciously considering what would be important to me as an "old woman."

> We have to learn wisdom.
>
> We have to learn to be financially secure.
>
> We have to learn to navigate relationships if close families is a value.

> We have to work at learning how to live any of our values well.
>
> We have to know what our values are if we are going to live life with a purpose.

How you treat people, how you spend your time, and what you say and do: These are all determined by your values. What you value is at the core of how you make decisions and what gives you purpose.

Refuse to Be Defined by What Happens to You

I remember a conversation with a man in his eighties. He had out-lived his wife of 50+ years. He had some health limitations—stiff joints, more weight than was easy to move, gout, and more. He was waning in his desire to live. "I'm not sure why I am still here," was his startling revelation.

This was a man with 20+ grandkids, 80+ years of knowledge, stories galore, humor that was entertaining, and history of interest to all, and yet, he felt no purpose.

Granted, he was not able to be as active as he once was. There were some parts of the world that seemed to be moving faster than he could keep up with. Many of the old tried-and-true resources that had worked for him had been replaced with technology that was beyond him.

However, I know there were members of his family who cared for him and deeply respected him and wanted to learn from him. A simple "well done" stated to those around him would have had an enormously positive effect. He could have purposefully empowered others with some intentional affirmation.

But he had not been able to find purpose after his wage-earning years, and then his husbanding years, were past. He became, unfortunately, a victim of his circumstances, defined by his age and limitations.

Rising above circumstances is not often simple, but it is almost always an option. There are tons of examples of people who lived well after tragic accidents or unfortunate life events or unwelcome changes. We know them in our circles of friends. We read about them as well. Following are a few examples I can think of, off hand.

❧ ❧ ❧

I have a client/friend who had a horrendous experience with a husband who had a brain tumor that altered his personality towards violence. They were high school sweethearts, happily married when he radically changed. The tumor wasn't discovered until their marriage had been ruined, their children scarred, and his life tragically ended. She told me the story after I already knew her as a happily remarried grandmother and valued business woman.

❧ ❧ ❧

Another newer friend in her late seventies has told me of her two ex-marriages. One was to an abusive man whom she found the strength to leave with their young son. The other was seemingly happy until he abruptly left for his ex-wife after my friend had raised the other couples' five children. He fairly-quickly realized he regretted his decision but the damage was done and she was not to be taken in again. "It wasn't so bad. I got rid of 5 teen-aged kids," she quips.

She later provided her mother with a home and good nursing care after she had suffered a number of strokes and other difficult physical illnesses. What does she do now? Cooks and bakes for her friends, cares for her 1-acre property, and maintains at least one rental property—always with an eager eye out for someone who needs her help.

❧ ❧ ❧

We live in a town with a university that has an important wheelchair sports community. It is common to come up on a group of athletes in wheelchairs on country roads, building stamina and honing their skills. Boston Marathon winners, Para-Olympic medalists, champion basketball team members are common around town. These are truly inspirational examples of choosing to be identified intentionally by something other than "what happened to you."

❧ ❧ ❧

There are the bitter, angry ones who have severed relationships. There are the sorrowful, "woe is me" complainers who only can focus on their own pain or misfortune. There are the sad ones who give up when too much has changed.

Our lives are worth a lot, all the way to the end. With purpose, we can live well all the way to the end, no matter what our circumstances have been—or what they will become.

Intentionally Determine What You Want to Do

There are plenty of good examples of people who have been able to make something wonderful in their later years.

It's about wanting to do something, having a readiness to change, being willing to go a new direction.

- Author Frank McCourt took up writing at age sixty-five.
- Ronald Regan became president at age seventy.
- Actress Kathryn Joosten was almost sixty when she got her first role.
- Colonel Sanders hit KFC success at age sixty-five.
- Laura Ingalls Wilder didn't publish her first book until she was sixty-five.
- Grandma Moses was in her eighties when she first picked up a paint brush.

The list could go on and on—easily, thanks to the internet!

I have six grandkids with one on the way. I love them all (equally, of course). I am busy making sure a business is successful for myself and my colleagues. I'm starting another business. Oh, and I love to travel.

I love my grandkids and enjoy time when I am with them, but they sort of have to be scheduled in. A colleague of mine has children the ages of my grandchildren. She has a mother-in-law who did not have any help when her son was young and she wants to help her grandkids and their parents as much as possible. As a result, my young colleague is free to have a good career as an independent contractor in two different industries because her mother-in-law has a purpose of supporting her efforts by helping with the grandkids.

My colleague's mother-in-law and I, similar in age and in the same town with many of the same values, have very different purposes for how we use our time at this point.

We are each clear and satisfied and happy with where we are. Because we have each considered it and discovered what our purpose is at this stage of our lives. Even if we live into our nineties, life is too short to fill our time with things we don't like to do.

Find Deeper Meaning for Your Life

To have great purpose and to be sure that your life is worth living, you have to have a purpose greater than yourself.

A struggling substance abuser once was explaining the 12 Steps to a friend of mine. "You can make your Higher Power anything you want," she assured. "It could be that cardboard box over there."

I asked my son, who is active in a 12-Step program, if that was true. He, a master at diplomacy, said, "Usually it is helpful if your Higher Power has more power than you do." Wise words.

The Westminster Catechism states that, "Man's chief end is to glorify God, and to enjoy him forever." Ignatius said, "The glory of God is man fully alive."

There is a piece of having purpose that needs to settle the question of "why am I here?" at a basic level. Beyond wondering how to spend next weekend or who to schedule time with, a sense of worth, for self and others, needs a bedrock.

Finding a church to attend is a step to take.

Joining a Bible study is a possibility.

Engaging in conversation about the meaning of life with someone(s) you respect and admire is stimulating for the brain and the heart.

Understanding someone's journey using the 12 Steps can be enlightening.

Engaging a life coach or finding a good book on finding your purpose might help.

An honest search for something deeper than yourself will yield results. And it will give deeper purpose that you can hold onto, even if your circumstances change from what you desire.

As you intentionally become who you want to be…
KNOW YOUR PURPOSE!

Refuse to be defined by your circumstances.

Decide what your life is about.

Find deeper meaning.

CHAPTER NINE

DON'T GET STUCK

My mother was one of five children. They grew up in the Depression Era and had a life of scarcity for a long while. Her dad, a traveling salesman of baking supplies, dropped dead of some sort of heart event when he was in his thirties, I believe. Two of her siblings died in their fifties from heart related events. Another sister died from lung cancer, also too young. No one in my mother's family had lived past seventy-two, for as far back as anyone ever looked.

My father died at age sixty-one and he was the only love of my mother's life. It took her a few years, but she rallied to redecorate her home ("Now it is Martha's style," she asserted), to volunteer at several organizations, and to travel. She and her sisters took a number of fun trips while all were alive. After there were only two sisters, they continued to travel on—cruises, bus trips, even to Europe once.

My mother was retired and living a full life and enjoying herself and contributing to others. Things were fine until she reached her maximum life expectancy, based on her family's history.

On my mother's seventy-second birthday, she got up and got dressed, blew out her candles, ate her piece of birthday cake, and…sat down to wait to die. Everyone else in her family, both sides, back into all known history, had died by age seventy-two. In her mind, she would, too. So she sat down.

And got stuck.

Her phone calls were sad. Her activities didn't satisfy. Her life was less full. As I remember it, about two years after her seventy-second birthday, she called me and said (not in so many words), "Hey! I'm not dead yet!"

Indeed, she was not dead. She lived another twenty-two years after that ominous seventy-second birthday.

I'm not sure what woke her up, but one of the first things she did was plan a trip with her sister. They had a blast, and took a ton of photos that she organized into an annotated album. That album was revisited many times over the next twenty-two years. That was not their only trip, nor was it her only photo album! That trip was the beginning of years more of travel.

After deciding she would continue to live fully, she continued to volunteer at several places. She pushed wheelchairs for the "old people" at the hospital until in her late eighties, taught idioms to international students, and knitted blankets for babies in the neonatal intensive care unit, using yarn also wound into balls by "old people." (She complained to me that they could have been done better!)

My mother got stuck, but she didn't stay that way.

We all get stuck at some point.

But you don't have to stay stuck, either.

Know What "Stuck" Feels Like

Sometimes, being stuck, or in a rut, is not easy to recognize because it can come on quietly.

A rut has been defined as "a grave without ends." Fight the rut!

For me, feeling ill for a few days that then leads to a case of the flu can knock me out of my exercising routine and, very subtly, I forget that I was consistently making a trip to the gym a regular event. After that, it is really,

really, difficult to get back into that routine. I can begin to feel stuck in having low energy and doing nothing about it.

A night of feeling lonely can lead to feeling like you don't have friends and pretty soon, you are lonely all the time, because you forget that it is your responsibility to find people you enjoy being with.

Being stuck might feel like being sorry for yourself. When you are mopey inside, a rut can occur that can be a challenge to climb out of.

Here are some signs of being stuck that can help you identify what stuck feels like:

Resisting or ignoring any offers of adventure. (*Adventure: an unusual and exciting, typically hazardous, experience or activity.*) Maybe it's okay to leave off the "typically hazardous" part of that definition, but you get the idea! If you are never willing to try something new, if you are only doing the same activities over and over, or if you are not active in general, you might be stuck.

Don't be afraid of trying something just because you've never tried it before. Even if you don't want to repeat this particular adventure, having had the adventure will help you stay out of a rut.

In our local newspaper, there was a story about a man who is ninety-two years old, who has a bucket list. He sky-dived for his ninety-first birthday. At ninety-two, he wanted to white water raft—and he doesn't swim. He had a near-drowning experience as a child and has avoided water since. His family organized a weekend adventure that included white water rafting.

He was scared. He didn't like the raft pilot's detailed training about how to "avoid drowning" if he was thrown overboard, but he did it. He went on the white-water rafting adventure. According to the interview, he was "scared," "glad he did it," and "probably not going to do it again."

This is a man who will not get stuck!

Beginning to lose interest in new ideas or people or places. (*To lose interest in: become apathetic, to no longer like or enjoy.*)

I had two grandmothers. One of each "kind" of old woman. One (the "other kind of one"), whom we called "Grandma" died when I was about 12 years old. I remember her as strong in personality and weak in body. We visited her regularly, but it was usually not my favorite destination.

My other grandmother, the "nice" one, whom we called "Grandmother," I enjoyed. She was tiny, wore thick coke-bottle glasses and had a ready laugh.

But Grandmother did not allow us to bring anyone who was not family to her home. At Thanksgiving, only spouses were included—no boyfriends. At Christmas, only immediate family. Easter dinner, aunts, uncles, cousins, no one else. I don't remember my Grandmother having any friends at all, come to think of it.

After her last living sibling, a sister, passed away, Grandmother lived alone and depended on her three sons… then, two sons… then only son, my dad, to be her relational connections.

For years, when she was younger, this woman, probably 95 pounds dripping wet, all of 5 feet tall, mother of three, widowed twice, would board a Greyhound bus with a trunk of necessary belongings and travel more than 2000 miles between Austin, Texas to Seattle, Washington. Summers in the Northwest with her oldest son, winters in Central Texas with the other two sons and their families.

She was fearless and cheerful as she boarded that bus to head north. Dropping her off at the bus station, I was in awe of her spunk and eager anticipation. It seems to me that she always had a crossword puzzle book along to help the time (days) pass.

Each trip was an adventure. Her trunk arrived several weeks after she did, one year. No worries. She adapted.

At some point in her life, my Grandmother lost interest in meeting new people, lost interest in going new places, did not embrace new ideas. After my dad died, Grandmother lived on into her nineties, feeling alone and lonely, although she was loved, visited regularly, and had family around.

It was sad to see her shrink into herself. She definitely got stuck.

Being unhappy with your circumstances and complaining about it. There are so many sayings to remind us of the importance of our thoughts. And of our power to change the way we live our lives.

> *Change your thoughts and you change the world.*
>
> —Norman Vincent Peale

> *Only I can change my life. No one can do it for me.*
>
> —Carol Burnett

> *If you don't like something, change it. If you can't change it, change your attitude.*
>
> —Maya Angelou

> *If you change the way you look at things, the things you look at change.*
>
> —Wayne Dyer

> *They say that time changes things, but you actually have to change them yourself.*
>
> —Andy Warhol

Nothing happening? Start a book club or knitting group or write a letter to someone.

No one inviting you? Invite someone to your home for a meal or out for a walk.

Feeling bored? Sign up for a class.

Wishing you had seen the latest movie? Go alone.

Thinking you can't have adventures or you only want to be in familiar situations or complaining about the hand you've been dealt are sure signs you may be stuck.

If being unhappy is a rut you are in, maybe an experienced and skillful therapist can help you find your way out.

Take some action! Any action! Don't stay stuck!

Have a Clear Destination

In one of my team building adventures, I purchased an experiential training product called "Virtual World." It was best as an outdoor activity with a challenge for teams to use compasses and linear measuring to arrive together at certain locations for rewards (or consequences).

The teams needed to learn orienteering, which is using a compass to navigate over "rough country" (according to Webster). It was always helpful if there was a past Boy Scout or Girl Scout on the team. But, we facilitators could instruct in the basics of using a compass.

After the basics of finding north and doing the math to find the correct heading, the instructions were,

> *"Find your coordinates and then head that direction."*

A key part of getting to the correct spot was to find a stationary object (tree, telephone pole, roof point) and head there. Focus on that one spot. That one, immoveable focal point, called an *azimuth.* If you head out in a direction, looking down at your compass, you will, for sure, veer off course. If you fix your eyes on that non-moving, stable object, your azimuth, you have a much better chance of getting to where you want to go.

To keep from getting stuck in life, you have to know what you are aiming for.

You need to have a "life azimuth" that you can keep your eyes on.

This is not so easy for a lot of us.

We spend a lot of life, especially in our SecondThird (ages 30–60), heading where we HAVE to be. It can be tempting to think that our life will always be like that—defined by schedules that we have little control over.

Truth is, you have more control than you think and with some thought and intention, you can make sure your life is headed in the direction you desire, even if there are some side-trips or detours.

Taking a day to re-orient your direction is a great use of time.

> Go to a favorite spot—park, coffee shop, library, lake.
>
> Carve out some time to focus in (again) on where you want to end up, what you want to accomplish, who you want to be.
>
> What do you enjoy?
>
> Who do you enjoy?
>
> Where do want to visit?
>
> Who do you want to spend some time with?
>
> Who should you pursue (or avoid)?
>
> What do you want to learn?

Knowing where you want to end up will get you somewhere. But, if you head out without a clear focus on where you want to end up, you might end up being stuck. Heading out without an azimuth or focal point might feel like:

> ...wanting people to do things with you, but without the relationships that you will enjoy. Invest in those relationships now, even if you are limited with how much time you can give.
>
> ...resentment of being the go-to person, when you have let others let you do it all. Learn about and practice boundaries in relationships.

> ...wishing you felt more intellectually challenged, then realizing that you have been waiting for someone to invite you instead of taking some initiative for yourself.

Look for ways and/or places to offer your services or insight. You have to remind yourself often of what you are aiming at, then keep your eyes focused on that immovable goal. Avoid looking down, looking at steps, and keep the azimuth as your goal.

Maybe your destination is making a new friends, like my mother did. Maybe you need to ease out of a relationship that is one-sided and draining. Maybe your destination can be a class at the community college, or becoming a mentor, or inviting friends over to try your new recipes.

Knowing where you are headed gives purpose.

Having a destination can keep you moving forward to avoid getting stuck. A destination of living on purpose and with intention requires that you know where you want to end up:

> With family and friends who love you and you love them back.
>
> With interests that hold your thoughts and curiosity.
>
> With energy to stay strong and healthy.
>
> With care and concern for others besides yourself.

A life that is lived fully all the way to the very end.

Being stuck with no direction is easily remedied. Find your focal point, your azimuth. Define your future destination.

Let Others Motivate You

As mentioned earlier, when my mother was in her seventies she was living at home, getting her hair done weekly, eating out with friends regularly, attending "widow's night," pushing wheelchairs at the hospital, teaching idioms, and traveling.

She would drive a thousand miles to visit my family at least once a year. One year, she had a new car and one of my sons asked her how fast it would go. "I got it to 85 on the highway coming up here." Yikes!

When she was in her eighties she slowed down a bit. Her friends were slowing down, too. Some of them were ill and a few had died.

One day, in her mid-to-late-eighties, she was lamenting her friends' lack of availability. She had always been one of the instigators for her circle of friends. She was the chauffeur for many occasions. Now, she had fewer women who could (or would) venture out with her.

On a phone call when she was bordering on feeling sorry for herself, I said, "Well, Mother, maybe you need to find some younger friends."

And, so she did!

Maybe it wasn't the most compassionate response from me, but it got her unstuck. My mother actually told me that she went out looking for some new and younger friends and had thrilled one woman (in her sixties) with an invitation to go with her to an art and quilt show.

She let me motivate her to take action instead of feeling sorry for herself. And she kept gathering new friends for her entire ninety-four years!

You can also use the critical or negative thoughts you have to motivate you to change. You can use another one of my mantras. My husband and I call it, "You spot it, you got it."

"You spot it, You got it" is a gentle reminder that being critical of someone else is often shining a big, bright spot light on a personal area of need in yourself.

Somewhere back in my childhood, I remember an instance when I was critical of a friend's approach toward another person. My mother pointed out to me that usually, what you notice as a deficit in others is probably a deficit in yourself.

Ouch. I remember at the time reacting to that, confidently stating that I didn't have the annoying character defect I noticed in my friend. Of course, privately in my own thoughts later, I could clearly see that my mother was right.

This is a principle that I have not been able to forget. I have passed it on to others and have used it for my own self-improvement, letting my occasional 20/20 insight into others' lives be mirrored back to benefit my own growth.

Here's an example: Lateness is an irritating habit in other people that I have to constantly monitor in my own life. I like to function in a world where schedules and time tables are flexible, 10:00 a.m. meaning, "somewhere soon after 10:00 a.m." Or, Tuesday meaning, "Tuesday, unless something pushes it to Wednesday." Birthday cards sent and received within a month of the actual date count in my world.

At the same time, I can be highly offended when others are late to meet me. Unless I am hypervigilant of my core belief that other people have great significance, it can really annoy me. Especially if I have managed to make it on time! I can effectively, from my own perspective, justify my own tardiness—if I am not considering this principle of "You spot it, You got it!"

When I am annoyed to find that my keys or pen are "missing," I usually find all sorts of things that others have left out in the wrong places that are even more annoying to me than my own missing items.

I can stay annoyed, or I can use "You spot it, you got it" as motivation to have a place for everything—and to remind myself to put everything in its place when I am finished with it.

"You spot it, you got it," is a great motivator to consider others and to do the right thing. For instance, if meandering staff meetings make me dread every time I must meet with my fellow employees, "You spot it, you got it" will motivate me to be prepared and conscious of others' time when I need to call a meeting.

Pick an annoying habit of someone in your office or family. I would guess that it is either something that you do yourself or something that you used to do and had to learn not to do.

My husband travels quite a bit. When he is home, I am pretty sure that the dishes left on the counter or the towels on the floor of the bathroom are his, and only his, fault. Until he is gone, and I see dishes on the counter and shoes in the middle of the living room that are, obviously, not his.

Does "someone" not return borrowed items quickly enough (or at all)? Honestly consider your own lifetime record for returning borrowed items.

If personal phone calls taken by someone you are meeting with is a button-pusher irritation to you, you might check to see how often you are actually making phone calls that are not directly related to your business.

It is often (usually?) easier to spot the truth in others than it is in ourselves. Remember that adage about when you are pointing at someone else, there are three fingers pointing right back at yourself? You spot it, you got it. It is a principle that I have not been able to forget.

Letting others motivate me in this unspoken way helps me see who I do NOT want to be. When I feel critical, I try to take a step back and ponder how I might be seeing myself reflected in that other person. And I gently remind myself that "you spot it, you got it."

If you have a friend who is a constant complainer and you can't help but notice, there is a good chance you are a complainer to someone else. If you easily spot (and are slightly annoyed by) the person who demands to be the center of attention, you just might have the same tendency. If there is a habit or behavior that you quickly pick up on and react to in others, chances are it is a quality that you, yourself, are demonstrating to others.

This approach of seeing and admitting that we, ourselves, might be annoying, can help us build empathy and to be kinder to those around us. "You spot it, you got it" is a way to let others motivate us to change, for the better.

If you can remember "You spot it, you (probably) got it," it can help you to keep changing, keep improving yourself and making adjustments so you are pleasant to be around. Making changes from the annoying aspects of what you see in others can motivate you to keep from getting stuck.

❧ ❧ ❧

Being stuck is "being caught or held in a position so that you can't move."

Refuse to stay stuck. Don't start thinking that what you have experienced is all there is.

Keep your eyes open for people to meet and places to visit and experiences to have.

Be aware of ways you might be motivated to change by using "You spot it, You got it."

As you intentionally become who you want to be…
DON'T GET STUCK!

Know what STUCK feels like.

Have a clear destination.

Let others motivate you.

CHAPTER 10

SO…WHICH OLD WOMAN WILL YOU BE?

What changes are you willing to make now to ensure that your ThirdThird is your BEST Third?

Assuming there are thirty more years to live after we turn sixty, there is a lot to think about in regard to what you will be like in your ThirdThird as you grow "old." By the time we get to our ThirdThird, two-thirds of our life is past and there are no do-overs.

Who we are,
what we are like,
how others enjoy or avoid us
is only one small part of the challenge.

We have to consider and plan for what we want our lives to be like going forward.

Besides the Do's and Don'ts in this book, there are other questions….

Where do you want to live?
What do you want to be able to do?
Who do you want to do it with?
How do you build a lifestyle that gives you meaning and joy?

By living on purpose and making intentional decisions, you can invest in a ThirdThird that has meaning and fulfillment and that you look forward to in your SecondThird or even your FirstThird.

So, as you approach your ThirdThird, you get to choose:

> Give up and give in and take what comes our way.
>
> or
>
> Take control, decide what you want, and begin to ensure that the ThirdThird is the very BEST Third of your life.

The truth is that we have a lot of control over how that ThirdThird turns out, no matter which Third we are in. If we are introduced to the reality of living longer early enough, we can make life-style changes and can plan for some practicalities.

❧ ❧ ❧

Habits started early are the easiest ones to keep. For instance, physical habits. Paying attention to our bodies, so we are fit and active in our earlier years will pay off big in the ThirdThird. If you avoid fast food and easy-to-grab, sugar-loaded snacks in your SecondThird, there will be huge benefits in your ThirdThird: fewer medications, more options for activity, less time spent complaining about how you feel, easier weight control, better sleep and better teeth.

If adopting good habits for our physical health starts early, it is much, much easier to stay fit and active in the ThirdThird.

You should also review your financial habits. If you can view your resources as tools and not entitlements, you can avoid a lot of stress and fear about your ThirdThird.

Learn to use your resources wisely, saving and investing, living within your means in your SecondThird. It will bring huge benefits to your ThirdThird. Living within your means might take some discipline, foregoing some splurges you see others making. But if you avoid the slippery slope of credit, you will be way ahead as you enter your ThirdThird.

The outcome of a habit of self-discipline in regard to money might mean that in your ThirdThird, you have less stress, more options for where you live, opportunities to travel, and greater ways to give and share with others.

❧ ❧ ❧

Life goes quickly and it can feel like the ThirdThird shows up sooner rather than later. There is no need to dread it. Life can and should be enjoyable for a lot of years after age 60. In the FirstThird of our lives, we mainly learn.

We learn to walk and talk,
to count and to read,
to think for ourselves and to get along with others.

We learn to navigate relationships,
we learn that everyone is different (yet the same),
and we learn that there is give and take in life.

In the SecondThird of our lives, we mainly Earn. We spend a lot of our time in ages 30–60 earning a salary. Earning a reputation. Earning love and devotion. And earning wisdom and lessons from mistakes and successes. The SecondThird is when careers are defined, families are nurtured, and when our lives often feel as if they are not really "ours."

Our decisions here, in the SecondThird, are at the core of what we will be like in our ThirdThird. The SecondThird offers great opportunities to really begin to know yourself at a deep level and to be able to accept yourself at the core of your being.

Invest a bit of work in your SecondThird to understand yourself and you are well on your way to making your ThirdThird your BEST Third.

❧ ❧ ❧

Understand Yourself

Wiring

One of the most important investments in this SecondThird is to invest the time into knowing yourself well. You are wired uniquely and if you can learn and internalize and embrace the nuances of your beautiful internal wiring, the way you function best and with the most ease, you will do well.

When I was first introduced to a "personality test" or Behavior Style Assessment, I was searching for something solid to stand on. I was in an environment where I often felt misunderstood and like I just did not fit with the expectations I felt others had of me. When I found there were tools for self-discovery and understanding oneself, I was eager to learn about myself.

I jumped in with both feet and researched and read and listened and began to see that I was not "wrong," though maybe I was "different" from others in my fairly small group of peers. As I dug in, I found that I actually did "fit" in some categories, that I was "on the chart," that there was a way to describe some of my inner preferences and leanings.

I began to understand that I prefer a faster pace and that I like a challenge and that I'd rather do something than talk about it and that while I don't enjoy conflict (at all), I sometimes just have to state my opinions.

From understanding my wiring, I know that I am energized by a task, become critical and fault-finding when I am under stress, and that I fear being taken advantage of. I also have come to understand that I often appear to be more confident that I feel, but that it is probably best to just go with that and see if I can make it work for everyone.

Understanding my wiring is just about the most important investment I have ever made in myself.

Love Language

Beyond my wiring, I also know that the best way for me to feel loved is when someone is willing to spend quality time with me. I know that my husband expresses love to me by doing "acts of kindness" for me. So when he washes the dishes for me (instead of sitting down and listening intently to how my day was), I can feel loved, if I am willing to "hear" it in my husband's best language.

It was handy for me when I was diving into learning about the languages of love that of our five children, each of them had a different one of the five love languages as explained in the book with that title by Gary Chapman. I could see the different responses when I thoughtfully loved each child in the way they best could "hear" my love.

> One wanted to spend time together.
>
> Another felt loved with gifts (even if they were new socks, presented well).
>
> One needed to hear, with words, that he was loved.
>
> One shares the "acts of kindness" language.
>
> And one hears best through an authentic hug, physical touch.

Learning my own language and then beginning to be somewhat fluent (thoughtful) in expressing love to the people around me makes me able to love better in my ThirdThird.

Learning Style

My husband and I are about to begin a project of building a home by the river. We have owned this land for a long time, a wonderful gift of a place that we pinch ourselves to believe we own. As we consider our ThirdThird, we realize that a quiet, away place in nature and with opportunities for hiking and kayaking will be good for our souls. We also know that we both enjoy being hospitable and welcoming people into our home for good food and fellowship. And, we like a project.

So, we are planning and talking and drawing and getting advice and estimates. While my husband is sketching and measuring and planning on paper, I am wandering and pacing and imagining.

I need to be in the space. I need to walk there and imagine being there. Spray paint on the ground works well for me. Touching countertops is good for me. Standing in a room the same size as the room we are planning helps me. I believe some would identify me as being "kinesthetic" in my learning style.

I am also linear and concrete in my thinking. A bit black-and-white, and logical and neat and tidy (in my thinking). Algebra more than geometry. Crosswords more than jigsaws. Flowcharts more than spreadsheets.

I have learned to slow down and to take deep breaths and listen carefully when I am trying to communicate with someone who is more random and abstract.

❧ ❧ ❧

It takes some work and some time to learn to know yourself well, but it's worth it.

We usually know what we prefer to eat or drink, what colors we prefer, who we enjoy being around, the entertainment we like. Going deeper to understand what makes you tick at a core level is worth the effort. My experienced advice is to invest the time and, maybe money, in understanding yourself.

Others will try to define you. If you are not intentional about understanding yourself, you can lose yourself in those other definitions and expectations.

Besides letting others define us, another limiting influence is that when we are not living on purpose, not being intentional, we tend to think (when we are not thinking) that everyone around us is the same as us.

That limits all of us.

I remember, once, after taking a fairly-detailed and careful assessment that was being used in my community of friends, I told a friend I had discovered my behavior style. After I told her my results, she said, "No you aren't! You can't be that mix of those styles."

Somehow, she seemed to believe that she knew me better than I knew myself. That was not a relationship that lasted, unfortunately. I needed someone who would help me discover who I am at my core being, deeply and effectively and honestly, not someone who defined me with her own limitations and opinions.

As I have worked to understand myself, deeply and effectively and honestly, I have been able to place myself in situations that give me energy, that allow me to contribute generously, that give me reason to smile, and that make me deeply grateful and satisfied.

I have been able to remove myself from situations that wore me down, to move away from relationships that drained my energy, and to rid myself of guilt for having preferences and ways of seeing things.

❧ ❧ ❧

Those two "old women" in the nursing home back in 1980 gave me pause.

> One was "nice" and made me (and others) want to be around her.
>
> The other was "not nice" and made me (and others) want to avoid her.

As I continue to become the "old woman" I will be, it is my sincere hope that I will be someone who others not just want to be around, but someone who lives life with full purpose to the end.

An old woman who....
contributes and cares,
gives and shares,
experiences and enjoys,
teaches and learns,
encourages and inspires.

Which old woman (or man) will you be? With less energy to pretend, with less concern of how you are perceived, you will simply become more of who you have always been on the inside, at your core.

You get to decide!

Start being that person that you want to be today! Choose one of the Do's or Don'ts from this book and begin to make it yours. Then, choose another.

And let it change you.

Determine to live on purpose.

Start being that Old Woman you want to become.

QUIZ: WHICH OLD WOMAN WILL YOU BE?

1. A child picks the flowers out of your garden. You…
   a. Believe that beauty should be shared.
   b. Tell the child to ask next time.
   c. Tell the kid's mom you'd appreciate an apology.
   d. Yell "Get off my lawn!"

2. Someone cuts you off in traffic. You…
   a. Remind yourself you've done that, too.
   b. Slow down, let it go.
   c. Bad words come but are kept in your own car.
   d. Honk and give the one-finger wave.

3. There is one piece of yummy, chocolate cake left. You…
   a. Insist that someone else eat it.
   b. Split it and take the smallest piece for yourself.
   c. Split it and keep the largest piece for yourself.
   d. Wait until you're alone and eat it. And gloat.

4. Someone younger than you offers to help you unnecessarily. You…
   a. Let them help, thank them, and give them a tip.
   b. Say thank you, explain you can do it yourself, and give them a hug.
   c. Explain to them that you don't need help.
   d. Let them do it and give them more to do for you.

5. You are interrupted during your favorite television show. You…
   a. Stop watching because you believe that people are more important than tv.
   b. Ask them to wait until the next commercial.
   c. Tell them they'll have to wait to talk to you.
   d. Say, "I'm watching my show" and go back to it.

6. Family wants to change the traditional holiday celebration. You…
   a. Agree to fit with everyone else.
   b. Ask for options and assure all that you will be fine.
   c. Say you will adapt, if that is your only option.
   d. Keep to your own traditions, even if it means you are alone.

7. The conversations turns to politics. You…
   a. Make more coffee and pass the cookies around.
   b. Ask if the conversation can stay pleasant.
   c. Share your opinions, even if they are contrary to others'.
   d. State your opinion with conviction and leave no room for discussion.

Results

Mostly "a": Nice / Warm and loving

Mostly "b": Sort of Nice / Tolerant and pleasant

Mostly "c": Sort of Grumpy / Family will let you know when they are getting together

Mostly "d": Grumpy / People give you space

ABOUT THE AUTHOR

Debbie Hensleigh is in her "ThirdThird" of life and making it the best she possibly can. Building on her experiences as long-time wife to a man on his third career, a mother and home schooler of 5, earth-mother of sorts who used to grind flour to bake bread, and a serial entrepreneur (think Lamaze classes, basket weaving, ropes courses, team building, business coaching, and real estate), she is focused now on helping others design their own BEST ThirdThird.

Debbie is a speaker and writer. She blogs at *YourBESTThirdThird.com* and leads workshops, encouraging people to build on their FirstThird (when we learn), and their SecondThird, (when we earn), to design a life on purpose leading to their BEST ThirdThird.

IF she were to get a tattoo, it would be "grace" on her left wrist and "truth" and her right wrist. Grace and Truth is what she is intentionally learning so that when she is too old to pretend, what oozes out of her will bless and encourage others.

For information on hiring Debbie or to see resources for your BEST ThirdThird, visit www.YourBESTThirdThird.com.

Made in the USA
Monee, IL
22 April 2022